THAT ERA

AN UNFORGETTABLE MEMORY

PRACHI S. VYAS

Contents

Preface

This book is on an account of the year 2020, when the whole world was facing through the virus, all the chapters with incident are on a true based event. Even the pictures posted are from the cuttings of newspaper of 2020. All the experiences mentioned in the chapter are event based and many of them are my own experience. This book is all about the time period of the year 2020 and the difficult time of the quarantine. This is a non-fictious and a true event written book.

THE AUTHOR,

PRACHI S. VYAS

Contents

1

CH:1 THE BEGINNING

❤

November,2019

The whole India was decorating their homes, making rangolis, lighting diyas, hanging torans, purchasing sweets and fire crackers, visiting each other and wishing each other, celebrating 'Diwali' with family, friends, loved ones and our favourite- cousins.

Diwali, full of happiness, the whole country was enjoying but...

But, the year 2020- it wasn't happy and so...

It was night time...umm...around 9:15 or a round figure, my family and I were having our dinner when the news showed...No!! actually shouted.

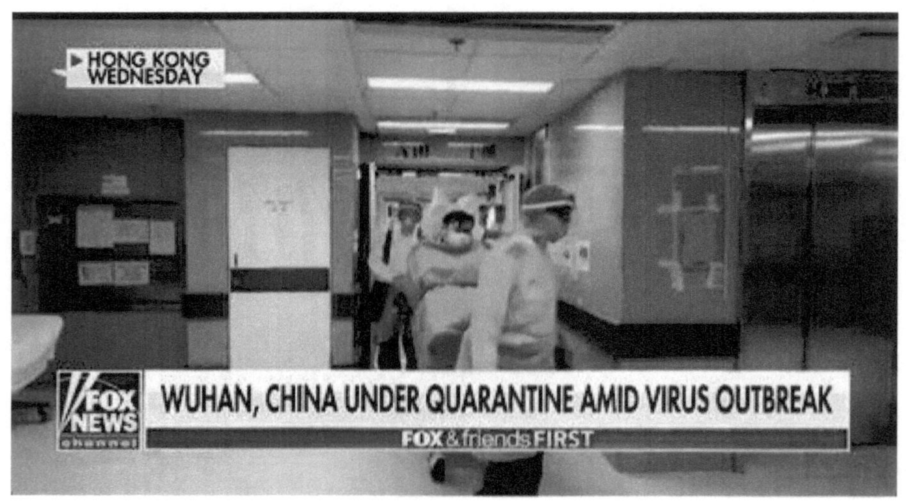

Quarantine in China(Wuhan)

Badi khabar, China se aa rahi hai ek badi khabar...and my mind struck- this China people never gonna change, again Indo-China battle(a small one).

But, no, I was wrong, this time it was not a battle, this time it was virus...Yes, ofcourse, CORONA:COVID-19.

(Laughing) and my hands upon my head...yarr!!! this was the news and they were shouting like nothing.

(Next day) all busy with thier works but dont't forget this is India, untill we don't discuss the news and criticise about it...we don't leave the topic.

We tution friends did the same, after the tution got over, like everyday we sat together...and the conversation started;

Khushi- Yarr tum logo ne kal news dekha....woh kuch toh China me naya virus aaya hai.

Me- Haaa....woh corona vorona aisa kuch naam hai.

Anarav- But suna hai ki yeh virus itna dangerous nai hai and touch karne pe bhi spread nai ho raha and slow spread ho raha hai.

Khushie'Me- Haaa...yeh aachi baat hai

Khushi- Chale ab, late ho raha hai, padai karni hai ghar jaake, warna boards ke exam ke time pe yeh corona nai aayega.(small laugh by everyone)

Exam cancelled due to Corona

On a serious note, in our discussion as Anarav told that corona is not spreading by touching he wasn't wrong at that time, as it was not detected that corona can spread through touch.

But(laughing) today when I look back and think I can't stop my laugh and at the same time amazed, Khushi, she just told in a laughing manner that corona will not give the exam and....

You might have listened- sometimes Goddess Saraswati comes and sits upon our tongue.

I feel the same, as in March,2020, the board exams were literally cancelled because of this corona. Making a history.

As the board exams were never ever cancelled in one's life...

Not a time passed by when....

2

CH:2 THE WARNING

December, 2019

Morning time and the watch was facing 7:00AM.

Everyone waiting for night...waiting to welcome new year with spread hands and thanking the year 2019 for being a good and memorable year. Bu..but, everyone were unknown of the dangerous upcoming year 2020 as it was not a year it was "the warning".

Happy New Year...yayy...wohoo!!!

Bye-bye 2019...tata tata...welcome 2020...happy new year.

year 2020

And everyone wishing each other, praying to God for a better year-bu..but this time God didn't listen.

Resolution of New Year;

January 1st, 2020.

But, it was completely the opposite in China, USA and many other countries...

As the corona had took many lives..more than thousand of death and the whole China locked-quarantined.

But, no one was interested atleast in India.

Woh kehte hai na- untill you yourself don't go through the same suffer the other is going through you would not feel the pain.

Same happened in India...it was all right till March.

Till the corona took place in India-

5th March,2020;

First case in India, a man residing in Kerala, came from abroad and he was suspected positive.

1,053 UNDER SCANNER IN STATE

IN INDIA	GLOBAL SCENARIO
➤ The woman from Kerala who tested positive for coronavirus **was hospitalised in an isolation ward in Thrissur** after returning from Chinese city of Wuhan	➤ China counts **170 virus deaths,** infection spreads to Philippines and South Korea. **7,711 people infected globally**
➤ She **developed symptoms of fever and a sore throat** and was quarantined along with four others in an isolation ward	➤ **Russia to shut border** with China
➤ **1,053 under surveillance** in **Kerala.** In **Hyderabad, 2 suspected cases** reported	➤ New cornavirus study places **incubation period around five days**
➤ **Sensex sheds 284 points** as virus scare spreads	

kerela report of corona

Wooho...and the news started;

Corona case in India...AAJ TAK, ABP, NDTV, India News, DD National only one news- A man at international airport was suspected positive and now is been quarantined in his home Kerala.

You won't believe but I have to surrender that for the first time I wasn't able to pronounce the word "quarantine".

Mene toh naam hi pehli baar suna tha..."quarantine"

Also, the must;

How can I forget that day, 11th of March,2020;

Oyyee...rang barse...rang barse bighe chunar wali rang barse..holi hai;

Dhuleti,2020

It's holi, festival of colours and joy...

But, this time it was a debet- should we play holi or not?

You won't believe but telling you honestly I was having my 10th boards exam, but still I was not ready to miss the opportunity of playing holi, untill it was society person itself to cancel holi.

Neverthless;

When all the gates are closed only one door, everytime open GOD-

I prayed and he listened.

We were going to have holi and corona would be thinking like;

Yeh kya mazak chal raha hai...meri toh koi izzat hi nahi hai...everyone busy in playing holi.

Minee- corona wasn't able to hold his disrespect as till 17th of March,2020. The whole India was announced a high alert and boards exams were cancelled making a history.

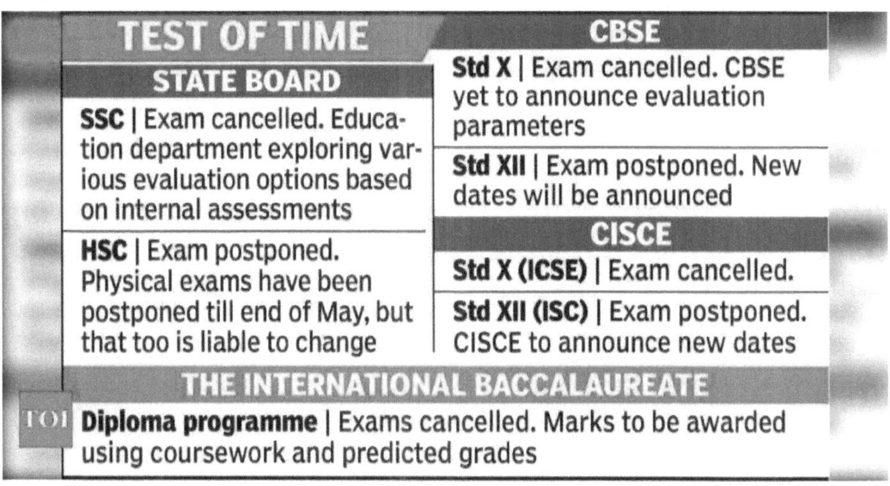

TEST OF TIME

STATE BOARD	CBSE
SSC | Exam cancelled. Education department exploring various evaluation options based on internal assessments	**Std X** | Exam cancelled. CBSE yet to announce evaluation parameters
	Std XII | Exam postponed. New dates will be announced
HSC | Exam postponed. Physical exams have been postponed till end of May, but that too is liable to change	**CISCE**
	Std X (ICSE) | Exam cancelled.
	Std XII (ISC) | Exam postponed. CISCE to announce new dates
THE INTERNATIONAL BACCALAUREATE	
Diploma programme | Exams cancelled. Marks to be awarded using coursework and predicted grades	

Exam cancelled due to covid-19

Not a day passed by and on 19th of March,2020.......

3

CH-3: LEVEL1--THE START

The clock making sound, still silent- due to the surrounding cheos. Dad was home, but his face was- a bit wierd than routine and there he ordered to turn onn the TV and put on the news.

I followed- turned on the TV and remote in my hand...my fingers dancing on the remote button. Ahh..ha 5..ummm 0, and last 4-504 and the news started.

Time-8:00PM.

Our Respected PM, Shri Narendra Modi were live and there he announced!!

Mere pyaare desh vasiyo, aaj raat 12'00 baje se sampurn bharat me lockdown ghoshit kiya jata hai.

Lockdown announcement by PM

(Slapping my head) Le...lag gayi...those were my words. You would be thinking why, sabki ki lag gayi, par kyuu?how??

As the announcement didn't only mean lockdown, it meant that all the shops, workship places, cinemas, school places, colleges, trains, airport, bus services...all are going to be closed.

public places were closed

Joh jaha hai wahi ruk jao...Bhale hi woh ghar phir rishte-daar ka ho ya dushman ka(laughing).

No service available accept medical and hospital.

Aree...ha..yaad aaya..I will share one incident;

One of our rishte-daar's relative had died and so, my cousin's aunt had visited there to give them sympathy. But, our PM had announced lockdown and the aunt who had visited to sympathise was struck there(laughing).

Matlab kya batau me aapko...agar koi najdeeki rishta hota toh chalta par relative ke bhi relative ke ghar pe struck.

GODD!!!

The year 2020 was not less than a history. Each month-week-day was making a history everytime.

The lockdown started and I can say with my whole gaurantee that it was after many years when all the family members were together and nor was it a sunday.(again creating a history).

1ˢᵗ day of lockdown, morning 7:30AM. I turned on the TV and started searching for DD National- to watch Ramayana.

Ramayana

If you remember during that lockdown the old devotional serials were back. Ramayana, Mahabharata, Shree Krishna, Chanakya,etc...

Shree Krishna

Waise, which was your mann-pasandita show?

While watching, my parents were recalling thier days and I can tight my pony and say that your parents too were recalling thier days and also your grand-parents.

Not only recalling thier days but also telling thier routine-they told me that on every sunday morning Ramayana was telecasted and due to unavailability of TV at thier homes, they used to go to thier nieghbour's home to watch Ramayana.

Also mentioned- at that time very few were having colour TV and so they had seen all the episodes of Ramayana black and white. I was able to feel it, yupp, not completely but yes partially.

Did you feel the same as I did, when your parents were telling you thier sunday morning routine?

Offoo, this morning went so fast, I wasn't able to live it completely...but at the other side I enjoyed it. Woohoo..mom has made tasty breakfast and all eating toghter- family that eats toghter stays toghter.(with a broad smile and looking ahead for amazing afternoon)....

4

CH-4 : QUARANTINE - THE FUN

It was afternoon time and watch pointing to 1:10PM, but no was having any work, even my mom had already completed with the kitchen work. We all were thinking what to do next-

which work..umm..kya kare ab?

I can say with my full confidence and facing up that this would have happened first time when all the family members(all together) weren't having a single work to do. Also, I can definetly say, same must have in your house...yes??

Suddenly, my brother spoke up-

Mumma-pappa chalo bussiness khelte hai...

We all noded to our heads to yes without any option left. It was around 1:30PM when we started playing-

Yayyy mujhe Indore mill gaya, hutt!! me jail chali gayi...I got Darjelling...Loll!!!teri ek chance skip...chalo-chjalo mere Rs.1300 lao...aree papa aap cheating kiye, haww!!chupke se paise le raha tha,chal chup-chap wapas rakh...

lockdown fun

Godd!! I will honestly say, the whole family playing together- sometimes argument, sometimes fuzzy but still- it's a very very heart touching feeling which can't be explained in words. Yes, those who might not have experienced this may think- ki game hi toh hai.

But, those who have experienced will feel the same..ya..some more or less, but yupp, would feel it. Now, tell me honestly, how many of you felt like I felt?

Still, whenever I recall those days- I start to laugh by myself..still doing soo.

Ohh God!! what to tell you we all were so busy playing the game that the time flew away and we didn't even know it. It was 4:30PM. We should now stop the game and also play something else, were the words of my dad...no-no, my mom added, I am having kitchen work. I will join from behind.

5:30PM- My brother with bat and ball in his hand, let's play cricket, ha-ha, aur koi kaam bhi kaha hai...(laughing).

We started to play and shouting- cheering and fun. Aree ha, one jaruri soochna;

Dad had given us one jaruri soochna, before the match started the ball should not go out of the main gate;

If the ball went out, the game will be stopped and not played again. The warning was not less than the PM Modi instructions for us.

7:00PM-

We all including mom, went to terris, there we were playing langdi-taang, santoli and also having talk together. But, to my amaze!! there was no was on the terris accept few families.

Lagta hai aaj kal log bhaut boring ho gaye hai..aree..ek ghanta chala gaya..it's 8:00PM. I think we should go down, said my parents. The sky was dark, twinkling stars and we all came down-

We all sat for dinner and before sitting I turned onn the TV for Ramayana as the time was already 9:00PM. Ramayana was completed, dinner was finished, what to do now, nind bhi nai aa rahi..

Ahhh...haa...let's play card-yes!!!

Phoo...now, what should I tell you, we started to play in an infinity manner. Started the game at 10:00PM and we ended the game at 2:20AM at night. Finally, after getting no winner, my parents ordered us to go to sleep.

*The night was silent and my mind was dancing inside-
the all day fun was not letting me sleep. Was your brain
dancing too??*

23

The next day...

5

CH-5: LOCKDOWN-A TASK

The next day, we followed with same routine of waking up than watching Ramayana. Mom completing with her kitchen work and we all with our works (cleaning the house and mopping the floor);

But that day, our PM were live to announce something important. As we all know, we were locked in our homes but still there were many warriors stepping out of the homes just for our security like our brave soldiers, the police workers, the doctors, the nurses, the social-servicers,etc...

That day, PM Modi announced the same, he encouraged the brave warriors and also requested us to encourage them.

He started,"Mere pyaare bhaiyo aur beheno me aap sab ko hardik nivedan karta hu ki aap iss mahamari ke samay me niyam ka paalan kare aur apne ghar me hi rahe aur hamare frontline warriors ka hosla badhaye, me chahta hu ki aap sab aaj shaam ko 6'00 baje ghar me rehkar hi hamare frontline warriors ka hosla badhaye, chamachh thali bajakar.

This all seemed funny to us, but this thali-chamachh, lighting of candles and diyas was very motiviting for the frontline bravers and gave them more power and courage to be dedicating towards thier work.

Lighting of diya during lockdown

Inspite we had a great loss, loss of time, loss of people, loss of economy, loss of everything we lost...

More than 1 crore cases, more than 5 lakh deaths, more thsn 50,000 people died due to lack of home, lack of food, lack of money, job...the graveyard was queued like a sale line, the ratio of death and graveyard was so imbalanced that people was burning thier own ones outside the graveyard.

Enter Caption

The year 2020 was a great destruction. All around corona, death, cases, and tabahi...not only the 2020 year but, the upcoming year......

Enter Caption